# PRINCE

# Prince

### D.L. Mabery

Lerner Publications Company
Minneapolis

LIBRARY OF CONGRESS CATALOGING IN PUBLICATION DATA

**Mabery, D. L.**
  Prince.

  Summary: A biography highlighting the career of the
popular performer and songwriter.
    1. Prince. 2. Rock musicians—Biography. [1. Prince.
2. Musicians. 3. Afro-Americans—Biography. 4. Rock
music] I. Title.
ML3930.P756M3   1985    784.5'4'00924 [B] [92]     84-26165
ISBN 0-8225-1603-9 (lib. bdg.)

    3  4  5  6  7  8  9  10  94  93  92  91  90  89  88  87  86

# Contents

# Success

Purple is Prince's color. Long before he named his first feature-length motion picture *Purple Rain*, Prince had adopted the royal color as his trademark. On his second album, *Prince*, which was released by Warner Brothers in 1979, his name is written in purple script, and a little purple heart dots the "i." In 1981 when he opened two concerts in Los Angeles for the Rolling Stones, the royal rocker wore a trench coat designed especially for him. On the shoulder was a leather-and-chrome-studded patch. And, of course, the coat was purple.

The cover artwork for his album *1999* is a psychedelic collage of purples. He rides a purple motorcycle and even lives in a purple house!

The man surrounded by all this purple, however, is more than just another movie star. As a musician, he is the individual credited with pioneering an entirely new musical sound, a fusion of many different musical styles. It combines the flash of techno-funk, as found in the music of Donna Summer, with the pure energy from rock 'n' roll, like Billy Idol. Then it adds the emotional feel of gospel, like Al Green or even Culture Club, and the snappy sing-along style of pop songs heard on the radio. Prince's music has a good beat and is easy to dance to.

The element that makes Prince's sound unique is the emphasis of the keyboards in his songs. The piano was the first musical instrument Prince mastered, and the songs he writes usually feature two keyboards: the electric organ and synthesizers. Where other musicians would use a saxophone or a trumpet in a song, Prince uses notes produced on the synthesizer. Unlike standard rock music, Prince's sound uses the guitar only sparingly. Most soul and funk music has a strong bass guitar line creating the rhythm. On most of Prince's albums, the rhythm section is created on the organ or piano by chords or with the electronic "clap" sound that a synthesizer can make.

In the late Seventies, this new musical style began to emit in waves from Minneapolis, reaching out across the nation. Not only was the nation hearing Prince's music, but they were hearing a number of other bands which imitated Prince's sound. It is not surprising that two of these bands, the Time and Vanity 6, were produced by Prince himself.

By the time *Purple Rain* was released, other American recording artists had also picked up on the Minneapolis sound. Ray Parker, Jr. used the idea for "I Still Can't Get Over Loving You" in the fall of 1983, and again for his Number One single, "Ghostbusters." Jermaine Jackson's 1984 dance hit, "Dynamite," was also heavily influenced by Prince's Minneapolis sound. For a whole new generation of music fans, Minneapolis became a mini-Motown, shaping the musical direction of the Eighties.

In addition to his musical talents, Prince has proven himself to be a superstar. With the release of *Purple Rain* late in the summer of 1984, he also became a movie star. Overnight, it seemed, kids all across America started copying Prince's way of dress. White ruffled-sleeved shirts and short-waisted jackets became popular, and boys and girls were cutting their hair short on the sides and long in the front like the Royal Highness of Rock.

The kind of star quality that Prince possesses does not develop overnight. It requires years of practice and dedication. And for Prince, the road to becoming a superstar has been a very rough one indeed.

# Prince's Story

The story of Prince is one of hardships. Early in life his parents divorced, and Prince moved from household to household until he was in high school. Prince missed growing up as part of a strong family unit. He lost the love and support of a family and, in particular, the security of having a father around.

Prince's real story begins in Minneapolis, the city in Minnesota where *Purple Rain* was filmed and where the club First Avenue & 7th Street Entry actually exists.

Prince was born in Minneapolis on June 7, 1958, and has one sister. His father, John L. Nelson, worked during the day as a plaster molder. In the evening, John Nelson played jazz piano for the Prince Rogers Trio. His wife, Mattie, had been a singer with the jazz group but quit when the couple got married.

In honor of the band, John and Mattie named their son Prince Roger Nelson. From his parents, Prince inherited his striking, doe-eyed dark looks. His father is a combination of black and Italian; Prince describes his mother as being "a mixture of a bunch of things."

For the first seven years of his life, Prince lived a normal, middle-class life. When he was seven, though, his family life changed. Prince's father moved out of the Nelson household, leaving behind his piano as well as his wife and children. For a long time, the piano became the only connection Prince would have with his father. Prince taught himself to play television theme songs on the keyboard. Before composing his own music, he picked out the tunes to *Batman* and *The Man from U.N.C.L.E.*

Next, Prince learned how to play the drums. "My first drum set was a box full of newspapers. The snare was the flap of the box," Prince remembers.

When his mother remarried, Prince found that he could not get along with his stepfather. Prince would later tell the minister who supervised youth activities at the local church how his stepfather once locked Prince in his room for six weeks. The only pieces of furniture in the room were a bed and a piano, and Prince passed the hours practicing chords and writing melodies.

Following this incident, Prince moved in briefly with his father, but after an argument he moved out again. This time he moved to an elderly aunt's home. It wasn't long before she booted him out for playing the guitar.

Prince's natural mother, Mattie, her children, and Prince's step-father attended the opening of *Purple Rain* in Los Angeles. Mattie, who was a singer, recognized Prince's musical talent early.

"I was constantly running from family to family," Prince has said of this troubled time during adolescence. "It was nice on one hand, because I always had a new family, but I didn't like being shuffled around. I was bitter for a while, but I adjusted."

At 13, Prince finally found a makeshift family to substitute for his own. He moved into the home of his best

André's mother, Bernadette Anderson, became a second mother to Prince. It was in the basement of this house that Prince and André practiced with their first band, Grand Central.

friend, André, whose family lived in a four-bedroom house on the north side of Minneapolis, across the Mississippi River from the skyscrapers and bright lights of downtown. André's mother, Bernadette Anderson, was a single mother raising six kids of her own. She was also attending classes at the University of Minnesota when Prince came to live with them.

To begin with, Prince shared a bedroom with his best friend, but it soon became apparent that the living habits of the two boys were very different. Prince liked to keep his room tidy, with everything in place. André didn't really care for housekeeping, and his room was a constant mess. So Prince ran a strip of tape across the floor, marking off his area, and told André to keep his mess on his own side. Finally, Prince couldn't bear it any longer and moved into the basement.

In the basement of the Anderson house, Prince quickly established his presence by fashioning a palace with mirrors and rabbit fur. Bernadette had little trouble with Prince. "He was a considerate, good kid who took turns mopping the floors," she remembers. Yet, even with six other children around, Prince never got too close to anyone. "He never talked about his mother and father. He kept a lot of feelings to himself," Bernadette has said. Prince still apppreciates Bernadette Anderson's generosity and, years after moving out on his own, he continues to send her a card each Mother's Day.

Prince was a loner during this time in his life. At school, he often sat alone to eat his lunch. He had very little money to spend—his only income was the $10-a-week allowance that his father was giving him. Bernadette housed and fed him but could not afford to give him any money. From his weekly allowance, Prince had to buy his school lunch and pay for bus fare. As rough as it was, he still managed to save money.

In the 10th grade, Prince tried out for the basketball team, following in the footsteps of his step-brother Duane. "Prince was an excellent basketball player. He was a good ball handler and could shoot the ball very well," recalls his coach at school. In spite of his five-foot,

**On the right is Prince as he appeared in his 1974 Central High School yearbook. At left is his stepbrother, Duane, who was in the same class.**

two-inch height, Prince made the junior varsity team. But it was perhaps the best team his high school had ever seen, and there were many other good players on the team besides Prince. That meant that Prince didn't get many chances to compete in the team's scheduled games. After sitting on the sidelines through most of the games that year, he quit the team in mid-season.

Prince's interest then turned completely to music. He spent most of his time in the music practice room, picking at the guitar or just listening to popular records. He was so involved in music that he hardly had time to develop friendships.

The only close friend Prince had during this time was André. Because both boys shared an interest in music, the pair had formed their first band when they were barely in their teens. Their musical partnership extended the family trees started by their fathers. Along with Prince's father, André's father had once played bass in the Prince Rogers Trio.

The first group the teenaged pals created was called Grand Central, named after the high school they attended. The band featured Prince on guitar, André on bass, Morris Day on drums, Linda Anderson (André's sister) on keyboards, and William Daughty on percussion. The group wore suedecloth suits with their zodiac signs stitched on the backs.

Grand Central practiced in Prince's basement room in the Anderson's red brick house. "It sounded like a lot of noise," André's mother recalls. "But after the first couple of years, I realized the seriousness of it." From listening to records by Grand Funk Railroad, Jimi Hendrix, Santana, and Sly Stone, Grand Central learned to play the mainstream rock that was popular at the time.

By the end of high school, Prince was well on his way to becoming a star. He had renamed his band Champagne and was writing all of its material. In his high school graduation program, Prince wrote that his future employment would be in music. Naturally, Prince was anxious to begin making records.

# In the Studio

In 1976, Champagne booked studio time at the Moon Sound recording studio in southeast Minneapolis, an area of town where the houses were larger and the yards a little nicer than the neighborhoods the kids in the band were used to.

The studio's owner was Chris Moon, a tall, good-looking man who spoke with a British accent. Chris worked at an ad agency during the day and ran Moon Sound in his spare time. Chris also had an interest in songwriting and had written several different sets of song lyrics. He needed a musical composer to create the tunes for his songs.

Soon after Champagne showed up at Moon Sound, Chris made a proposition to the shy young guitar player.

If Prince would write music for Chris' lyrics, Chris would give Prince and the band free studio time.

"I wrote down directions on how to operate the equipment, so he'd just follow the little chart," Chris has said, explaining how it was that Prince came to learn studio production and engineering techniques.

Over a period of eight months, Prince composed music for three songs, using the lyrics that Chris had written. He then recorded the songs, playing all the instruments himself. Another ad agency person, Owen Husney, heard the tapes and decided to manage the teenaged bundle of talent.

Owen Husney put together 15 press kits that included a demo tape of the three songs, pictures of Prince, and

**André Anderson, Prince's childhood friend, was in the band when Champagne went into Moon Sound Studios to record.**

a short biography of the musician. He headed off to Los Angeles to introduce Prince to the major record companies. Upon hearing Prince's work, CBS, A&M, and Warner Brothers all expressed interest in him. Husney, however, insisted to each record company that if Prince signed, he must be guaranteed the right to produce his own albums.

Warner Brothers Records, the company that eventually signed Prince, agreed to the arrangement outlined by Husney, but only on one condition. Prince must demonstrate his ability in the recording studio in front of three of their producers.

In the studio, Prince astonished the men with his knowledge. First he sat down at the drums and recorded the rhythm track for a song. Next he added the guitar parts, and finally, he added the keyboards. The recording industry men agreed that Prince had passed the test and gave him permission to begin recording and producing his first album, *For You*.

Released in 1978, *For You* was only a minor hit on the rhythm-and-blues charts. But because the 20-year-old Prince had virtually played all of the instruments and had sung all of the vocals, in addition to producing the record himself—a feat unheard of for a first record—the album did receive a lot of attention. The next year, Prince released his second album, titled simply *Prince*. It contained the song "I Want to Be Your Lover," which went all the way to Number One on the soul charts and firmly established Prince as a bright new recording artist.

# Recording Wizard

Back in Minneapolis, Prince put together a band to tour the country to promote his hit single. To play bass, he recruited his old friend André Anderson, who had by this time changed his name to André Cymone.

"There was a lot of pressure from my ex-buddies in other bands not to have white members in the band," Prince said later. "But I always wanted a band that was black and white. Half of the musicians I knew only listened to one type of music. That wasn't good enough for me."

**Prince and Dez Dickerson**

Prince's next album broke down a lot of the barriers between "white music" and "black music." Released in 1980, *Dirty Mind* mixed the funky dance tempos popular in black dance music with the straight-ahead heavy guitar attacks found in the rock 'n' roll of the white punk rockers. Although critics praised the album, Prince was booed off the stage in Los Angeles when he opened a show for the Rolling Stones.

Around the time that Prince started work on his fourth album, *Controversy*, a number of changes were happening in his life. First of all, André Cymone signed a recording contract with Columbia Records and left Prince's touring band. André was replaced by Mark Brown. Still backing Prince up on guitar was Dez Dickerson, who was to stay with the band for two more years.

Secondly, in addition to writing music for himself, Prince had begun to write and produce music for other groups. The first group of musicians he produced was Flyte Time, a band of rhythm and blues players. Flyte Time had been playing around the Minneapolis area for a couple of years. Prince changed their name to the Time and brought in Morris Day, who had been the drummer in Grand Central, to sing vocals on the album. For the Time, Prince wrote the song "Cool," which became a big dance favorite.

Later that same year, Prince auditioned three women singers for another group he had in mind. He named the group Vanity 6. Backed up musically by the Time, Vanity 6 sang disco songs written and arranged by Prince.

**Morris Day went from the Time to the big time after his role in** *Purple Rain.* **He moved to Hollywood, where he signed a three-picture movie contract and began working on his own solo album.**

With all this recording activity going on, Prince still managed to write new material to perform himself. In 1982 he released *1999*, a two-record set for which he had written, produced, and arranged all of the material.

When *1999* was completed, it yielded three hit singles: "1999," "Delirious," and "Little Red Corvette." Because of the popularity of the singles, the album sold nearly 3 million copies. *1999* became Prince's most successful recording project, and clearly indicated that the world was ready to listen to his brand of funky, danceable rock 'n' roll. Now he was ready to take on a new challenge, that of creating a feature-length motion picture. And the idea for *Purple Rain* was born.

# Making *Purple Rain*

When Prince decided to make a movie, he began looking around for a writer and director who could handle the project he had in mind. For over a year, Prince had been jotting down ideas in a purple notebook. What shape the movie would take was still unclear.

In Hollywood, Prince met with William Blinn, a seasoned scriptwriter, to discuss his project. Blinn had won television Emmy awards for his writing and was currently on summer break from the TV series "Fame," for which he was the executive producer. He therefore had time to concentrate on trying to turn Prince's vision into a script.

Prince was fairly vague about the plot of his movie. After seeing one of Prince's concerts in Minneapolis, Blinn met with Prince a second time. It was then that he discovered an important fact: part of the story that Prince wanted to tell in his movie had to do with his father, John Nelson.

Blinn began writing a script which he called *Dreams*. It was about a character whose parents are dead and who plays in a rock band. At Prince's request, Blinn changed the title to *Purple Rain* and finished the first draft of the script. When the fall season of "Fame" started, Blinn was called back to Los Angeles and left Prince's project behind.

Prince and his management team were uncertain about what to do next. They decided to look around for a director to work with Blinn's script. Someone recommended a young film editor, Al Magnoli, for the job, and they approached him. Al met with Prince over dinner to discuss the movie project in more detail. Afterwords, Prince looked at Al and said, "I don't get it. This is the first time I've met you, but you've told me more about what I've experienced than anyone in my life." Al had many suggestions for improving on the story line in Blinn's script and wound up rewriting it. In the end, Blinn and Magnoli shared the credit for the screenplay.

The filming of Prince's movie began in the fall of 1983. Olga Karlatos was chosen to play the mother, and Clarence Williams III, who had once played Linc on TV's "The Mod Squad," was cast as the father. Morris Day and the Time were also in the movie. Prince had planned originally to feature Miss Vanity of Vanity 6 playing opposite him. Shortly after the film went into production, Vanity dropped out of the project and was replaced by Patty Apollonia Kotero, a young Hispanic model from Santa Monica, California.

The movie was filmed in and around Minneapolis, using locations familiar to its star. Prince also put together a new band, the Revolution, to back him up for the concert scenes filmed in the First Avenue club.

On all of his previous albums, Prince had played all the instruments and had sung all the vocals. The only exception were some of the backup vocals used on the album *1999*. On the album *Purple Rain*, he used a band in the recording studio for the first time. That band, the Revolution, included both white and black musicians as well as two women.

# The Kid's Story

*Purple Rain* has been described by its creators as being "an emotional biography" about Prince's life. That is, while the events in the story may not have actually happened, the hopes and fears of the Kid, the leading character in the movie, are those of Prince. In *Purple Rain*, fact and fantasy overlap, creating a new rock 'n' roll legend.

In the film, the Kid is an up-and-coming musician who has put together a band called the Revolution. The Revolution plays live at First Avenue & 7th Street Entry, the town's most talked-about nightclub. The Revolution is popular, but the main attraction at First Avenue is a rhythm-and-blues act called the Time, led by Morris Day. Competition to headline at the club is intense, and conflicts erupt between the two band leaders.

On stage, the Kid is a confident showman. At home, though, his life is miserable. He is the only son of a black father and a white mother. His father was once a musician, too. In the basement of the Kid's house sits a piano that his father no longer plays. Frustrated by lack of success, the father drinks heavily and has frequent fights with the Kid's mother.

To escape his parents' fighting, the Kid has created his own private world in the basement of the family house. His room downstairs is filled with candles, masks, and momentos. Here he practices his guitar and spends time listening to tapes of his band on a cassette deck.

Onto the scene appears the beautiful Apollonia, a singer from New Orleans. She has been drawn to First Avenue in search of stardom. Although she is immediately attracted to the Kid, she eventually becomes taken in by Morris Day's lady-killing charm. After dating the Kid, Apollonia accepts an offer from Morris to sing vocals in an all-female band he is sponsoring. When the Kid finds out, he has a fight with Apollonia that is similar to the way in which his father fights with his mother.

Meanwhile, things are not going well with the Revolution. Wendy, the guitarist, and Lisa, the keyboard player, have written a song which they've submitted to the Kid for approval. However, he refuses to play any material

**In concert, rhythm guitarist Wendy Melvoin receives a playful hug from her boss. Wendy replaced Dez Dickerson when he left the Revolution in 1983.**

written by anyone other than himself. He appears to feel that the girls' songwriting efforts are an attempt to take over the band. Then, following a bad night on stage at the club, the manager of First Avenue tells the Kid, "Nobody digs your music but yourself." It seems that the Kid can do nothing right.

That night, the Kid comes home to find his mother sitting on the curb with a black eye. He rushes inside the house, angry enough to fight, only to find his father sitting alone, playing the piano. He is playing a song that he wrote, and the Kid asks to hear more. Knowing that their love for music is the only thing the Kid and his father have in common, the Kid hopes that it is the way he and his father might be able to understand one another. His father responds that, unlike the Kid, he never had to write any of his songs down. Instead, he says, they are all committed to his memory. When the Kid asks his father about the fight he had with his mother, the Kid's father gives his son some advice: "Don't ever get married."

Later in the movie, after his father has tried to kill himself, the Kid finds a trunk full of sheet music handwritten by his father. The Kid realizes that throughout his life his father was never able to admit his faults. He vows that this will not happen to him.

With the Revolution, the Kid returns to First Avenue for one last night, playing a song based on his father's music. He also plays the tune that Wendy and Lisa, the women in his band, had given him earlier. The set of songs is so emotionally charged that everyone in the club that night is dramatically touched. The movie ends with an uplifting scene as Apollonia leaves Morris for the Kid and the Revolution emerges as the true star band of First Avenue.

The moral of Prince's rock 'n' roll fable is clear. In order to find happiness, a person must first learn how to give—and receive—love.

# A Shy Superstar

Prince the superstar lives alone in a normal-looking, two-story house located in a wooded area on the shores of a quiet lake west of Minneapolis. There are no limousines parked in the driveway, no swimming pool in the yard, and no name on the mailbox. The house has four bedrooms and a basement which holds a recording studio. Like everything else Prince loves, the house is painted purple.

Prince also owns a warehouse out in the countryside near Minneapolis. There he conducts his business. Inside is an office, a rehearsal studio, a dance studio, a custom clothing shop, and a hair and makeup salon. Prince and the Revolution practice their concert show on a stage in the rehearsal studio. Installed in the studio are theater lights for the stage, and behind the stage is a backdrop that shows a silhouetted city skyline. This is the same backdrop used by the Time when they played on First Avenue's stage in the movie *Purple Rain.*

Beyond the rehearsal hall is the dance studio with wooden floors and a wall of full-length mirrors. Here is where Prince and his band study dance and practice the moves they will perform on stage. The walls of Prince's warehouse studios are draped with a purple satin fabric that reflects light differently from different angles. The coat Prince wears in the photograph inside the album *1999* is also made of this fabric.

When he is not at home or in the studio, Prince can be seen driving around the back streets of Minneapolis on the same purple motorcycle that is on the cover of the album *Purple Rain.* At other times, he is ushered downtown from his suburban home to the First Avenue club in his black BMW for an evening of dancing.

Despite the bad-boy, rock 'n' roll edge of Prince's image, Prince does not use either drugs or liquor. In fact, he is deeply religious. As a child, Prince attended a Seventh-Day Adventist church. To this day he reads the Bible regularly. Prince has even dedicated all of his albums to God.

In 1984, Prince began his six-month "Purple Rain" concert tour. As with all of his projects, Prince oversaw everything from the choreography to the stage design.

His "Purple Rain" tour gave Prince a chance to work for charity. He asked concertgoers in St. Paul, Minnesota to bring cans of food for the needy, and collected over 23 tons of food. He also played free concerts for disabled children, and insisted that he get no publicity for them. His generosity didn't end with the tour. A small Chicago school has received over $500,000 from him.

Since the success of *Purple Rain,* Prince has been offered other movie roles. But his second movie was another special project for him. In *Under the Cherry Moon,* released in 1986, Prince not only is the star, but also took over the director's job, and wrote, performed, and recorded the soundtrack music.

Prince's fans and his fellow musicians have shown that they admire his work. He has won numerous American Music Awards, given by a poll of 20,000 record buyers, and Grammys, awarded by an academy of 5,000 musicians.

Early in 1985, Prince announced that he was no longer going to tour. Soon after, he released *Around the World in a Day,* which quickly hit the top of the charts. *Parade,* music from *Under the Cherry Moon,* has shown that his popularity is not waning. Despite his overwhelming success, Prince remains as shy today as he was in high school.

## Photo Credits

Greg Helgeson: pp. 1, 2-3, 20, 25, 33, 40, and back cover.
Ebet Roberts: pp. 6, 10, and 36.
Peter C. Borsari/People Weekly ©1984 Time Inc.: p. 13.
Steve Kagan/People Weekly ©1984 Time Inc.: p. 14.
Minneapolis History Collection/Minneapolis Public Library: p. 16 (both).
Paul Natkin: pp. 18, 22, and front cover.